"From suburban streets to worldwide events, Jurkovic fights back with humor, ranging from dry to hilarious. Everything is political, and Jukovic doesn't care what you think. He'll keep writing dis-turbing notes and speak his mind. His new collection, *mooncussers*, provides entertaining lessons for us to emerge from the matrix that keeps our minds imprisoned."

> - Patricia Carragon— Curator/Editor in-chief Brownstone Poets, Brooklyn, NY, author of *Angel Fire* (Alien Buddha Press).

"*mooncussers* finds Jurkovic up on stage soloing all around and about the catastrophe, making big-hearted clever nudges to build another little machine of words, each offering the solace of company if not the surcease of sorrow."

> -William Seaton, poet, translator, critic, and former member of San Francisco's Cloud House group

"In these poems, Jurkovic plays his signature dark jazz of anxiety, irony, empathy. But his ear is tuned as well to rich tones of contemplation that stop us in our tracks: "the air, hushed, flawless; the river a hug of diamonds." He plays the whole keyboard with love and skill."

> - Irene O'Garden, Poet (*Fulcrum: Selected Poems*), Author (*Glad To Be Human*), Off- Broadway playwright (*Women On Fire*)

"In *mooncussers*, Jurkovic takes his readers on a journey that like the jazz he loves so well, combines music, words, and rhythm. He invites us to enjoy the world he so eagerly inhabits, a world that we know begins with easy conversations, but deceives, twisting and hitting out: "It's like all the flagmen / came out of hiding / . . . So imagine this mob at rush hour, / closing in for the kill." And yet the poet sees beauty down every street: "The air hushed, flawless. / The river a hug of diamonds."

> -Bertha Rogers, poet, *What Want Brings: New & Selected Poems*; founder, Bright Hill Press & Literary Center, Treadwell, NY

"Funny, outrageous, courageous, Mike Jurkovic's poems take risks, as if every choice the poet makes were a left turn at a busy intersection at rush hour. Innovative, arresting, his poems provoke and tease."

> -Dr. Lucia Cherciu, 2021 Dutchess County Poet Laureate, Professor Department of English SUNY / Dutchess

"A poet of intense precision, a collection of little daggers that head straight to the heart of things."

> -John Pielmeier— Playwright (*Agnes of God*), Screenwriter, Novelist (*Hook's Tale*)

mooncussers

Poems by Mike Jurkovic

Luchador Press
Big Tuna, TX

Copyright © Mike Jurkovic, 2021
First Edition: 1 3 5 7 9 10 8 6 4 2
ISBN: 978-1-952411-86-1
LCCN: 2021950600

Cover image: Emily Monahan / Mike Jurkovic
Author photo: Mike Jurkovic
All rights reserved. No part of this publication may be reproduced or transmitted in any form or by any means, electronic or mechanical, including photocopying, recording or by info retrieval system, without prior written permission from the author.

Acknowledgements:

"9/10s of Tuesday" - *Harbinger Asylum*, Spring 2021,

"Autumn's Blue Rain" - *Jerry Jazz Musician,* January 2021,
   Illuminations, June 2021,

"Ballad of Black Bean Johnson" - *Waymark -*
   Voices of the Valley # 17,

"Brubeck's Bar #6" - *Albany Poets,* Winter 2021,

"Brushing Light Snow" - *JerryJazz Musician,* Winter 2021,

"Gracie" - *Zingara Press,* 2020, *Home Planet News,* 2020,

"Hellfire and Fever" - *Stone,* Issue 2, November 2021,

"Ill-Fitting Suit" - *JerryJazz Musician*, Summer 2021,

"In the Grey Light" - *Home Planet News*, 2020,

"Left of the Green Lamp Shade" - *Main Street Rag*, Spring 2020,

"Swimming w/Picasso" - *Adelaide Magazine #22,* March 2020,
   Waymark – Voices of the Valley, #10,

"the hour before" - *Chronogram*, January 2021, *Panopolyzine,*
   Winter 2021,

"The Raw Edge" - *Stone,* Issue #2 November 2021,

"this." - *Chronogram*, November 2021,

"Walking Awosting" - *Shawanagunk Review,* Summer 2021,
   "where the light sneaks in" - *lightwoodpress*.com, Winter 2020,
   Zingara Press, Spring 2021,

"You, Blue Dice, & Squirrel" - *PoetryBay.* Winter 2022

Table of Contents

Wide Left Turns (crossing Cedar) / 1

Hellfire and Fever / 3

You, Blue Dice, and Squirrel / 4

this. / 5

Swimming w/Picasso / 6

Autumn's Blue Rain / 7

Fork misplaced. / 8

Gracie / 9

The Raw edge / 10

Not Wine / 11

Something other than / 12

Hat Check Girl / 13

Left of the Green Lampshade / 15

where the light sneaks in / 16

Combustible Flannel / 17

the hour before / 18

Two Miles North / 19

Legend Holds / 20

it was an evening / 21

The Reason You Dreamt (after ra) / 22

In the Grey Light / 23

flaws apparent / 24

Elephant, galleon, whips, and chains / 25

fuckin' town / 26

Brubeck's Bar #6 / 27

Brushing Light Snow / 28

Ill-Fitting Suit / 29

Pittsburg / 31

In a Walmart In Kentucky / 32

Scuff Marks / 33

Breaching Aristotle (month4) / 34

brushfire / 35

Ballad of Black Bean Johnson / 36

E suspended / 37

Liberal, Kansas / 38

Light Between Buildings / 39

Man w/the Giant Camera / 40

Eve / 41

Fuzzy Circles / 42

Shamed Angels / 43

in my car of feathers / 44

Fish Talk / 45

Data spill / 46

9/10's of Tuesday / 48

Walking Awosting / 49

The Merchant's Receipt / 50

suit of blue / 51

pissin' 'round the lilies / 52

Rejection 629 / 53

*Like America I've many bridges in disrepair.
These three, thankfully, remain intact.*

*To CAPS, for choosing community over discord,
and for keeping me honest*

*To my salon mates, JD, KH, RK, and GR
for making several of these possible*

To Emily for making it real

mooncussers

Wide Left Turns (*crossing Cedar*)

It's like we all couldn't wait
to get back in our cars and make
wide left turns. Roll through stop signs.
Drift the yellow. Brake! Speed. Stop! Signal.
Then turn the opposing way.

It's like we all never left
the driver's seat. Took our meals
in the garage lit by a sixty watt.
Schoolbus! Schoolbus!
Old mayhems anew.

It's like right lanes closing
in a quarter mile and
don't tail construction vehicles
okay? They got enough shit
going on at home
and don't need your bulwark
riding their ass.

It's like all the flagmen
came out of hiding:
Guys in trees and guys on poles.
Old lady Swenson crossing Cedar
for her mail.

It's like everyone now has a license
and a fix to fill and it's only noon!
So imagine this mob at rush hour,
closing in for the kill.

Hellfire and Fever

Unlike stories
of her acquiescence,
Buddha's wife
was all hot n bothered
n lookin to party.
I know. I was there.
She stood her ground
and made her rain
w/a ferocity
seen by few
and survived by less.

Day in, day out
that girl made wreck the priories,
Brought hellfire and fever
to government men.
Eyes straight. Head high.
Tits up. Her bangles
all a-jangle.
Her roguery legend 'round here.

Yaso (as we called her)
made her own revenge.
Taught her gentle charge
that all men are fickle
(most women too)
and that no man is better
than the other.

We all see the dark of day
so make yourself a light

You, Blue Dice, and Squirrel

If I gave a damn
I'd finish the poem
you commissioned
but I haven't the energy
to concoct
so elaborate
a lie
about
You, Blue Dice, and Squirrel
barrel assin' down
a swollen Mississippi
to save
Blind Boy Jim's
'27 National
from foreclosure
and your morally
preposterous
escape route.

How unsettling to know
I beg your fiction.
Explain myself
w/your errant words.

this.

Sugar n shit
　fall from the sky
　　and here
　　　I am
　　　　(four fingers in hand
　　　　　two sheets to the wind)
　　　　　not dire
　　　　　　nor enlightened.
　　　　　　　Prophet,
　　　　　　　nor fool.
　　　　　　　　Just some
　　　　　　　　hoary shaman
　　　　　　　who,
　　　　　　　once confronted
　　　　　　　and on a roll,
　　　　　　has more
　　　　　　than a few
　　　　　words to say
　　　　　and says them
　　　　something like
this.

Swimming w/Picasso

Swimming w/Picasso
was all fun and games
Until we both conceded
we couldn't swim
and everything
reassembled:
Arms. Legs.
Nipples akimbo!
Elbows. Eyebrows.
Monkfish cheeks.
Treble sevens. Dancing deer.
The bent dick of a zebra.

Maya Marie Olga Dora.
All of them reclining. Jutting nose.
Rolling eye. Ballerina mistress.
The punishment of art.

Shipwrecked cur that he was,
he set the beach afire. Siren scream.
Toddler dash. In his rampaging light,
I unmoored his shoddy boat
into the cursing tide,
Leaving him his brushes
and the wreckage of the sea.

Autumn's Blue Rain

Right before they shipped me off
to ports I inhabit still,
Mary, from sophomore year,
(who died this year from cancer of course)
told me as if, divining autumn's blue rain
drop by sad wet drop,
the sinner resides in the holy.

She always said so much w/so little,
artist that she was. And as I was swept into battle
both here and abroad, I carried her words w/me,
beyond the yearbook effect,
the goodbyes and so longs
of well-meaning friends, those who wished me gone
and family, too.

Then came the massacre at Hue and well,
here I am now: two doubles down,
awash in my clouds of logic. Wondering why
some make it and some don't and
how many bodies make up that bridge.
How many Marys have to die
to satisfy our penchant for regret
as autumn's blue rain chills
graves—ancient, barren, freshly dug.

Fork misplaced.

In the shanty hut of memory
I put down my things. Prepare tea,
a bowl of grain. Arrange my space
into the same order. Kitchen. Bedroom.
Bathroom. Den. A small room for secrets.
My desk skewing east. Bed aligned.
Shoes missing. Fork misplaced.

Gracie

There's a grammatical error up ahead
that will change everything. How and why
I don't know because,
off the top of my head
Each mad essay
must cast doubt
on the one before
Or at least lend a hand
to its abhorrent cause
Which makes for unsure seasons,
rising seas and a lack of wonder.
And I know you have better places to be
like Dunkin' D or debtors jail,
So I'll try to get to what I'm getting at
before I get to where I'm going,
Which was to talk about Gracie Allen
Who knew today's postage stamp
was yesterday's head of state.
That a country of checks and balances
relies on checks
And that you never place a comma
Where God has put a period.

The Raw Edge

w/o giving it all away
this one's a city narrative
about an apprentice seamstress
who makes the fine stitching
disappear. Cuts the bias
to the gain. Binds the anchor,
cords and feathers.

On the doorstop
of a long time,
she parts headstrong
the eastern winds
knowing each knot
has left her sure
of this: The pattern wherein
the raw edge crosses
the yardage and seam,
giving no inch more
than one deserves.

Not Wine

In any book of Manhattan dreams
shadows slant on Crooked Street.
St. Peter loiters the cashier's cage.
Your rifle's only as good as your scope.
The hungry open fire
not wine.

Something other than

Jack, the sailor's cat,
stares into the teapot.
The toaster. The tempest.
The chrome base of a lamp
from some other time of duress,
And is just as enamored
of his reflection
As any of us
would be
if only
we weren't
creatures of habit.
Enthralled by the shrapnel bell.
Escaping the ninth scrutiny
w/more alarm than faith.
Setting off, like Artemis,
into a season of
few remaining days.

Hat Check Girl

You always tip
the hat check girl
whose reliable witness
you'll need sooner
than you know.

Whose bright wide eyes
(yon cisterns of dream)
uphold your dignity
in spite of your totem,
your tarry

Your existential quiddities
and false drawings.
All the camo
the day demands.
Expects.

Culls cold.
Leaves w/o kiss
or condemnation.
Only your vain schematics
at play.

You always tip,
the hat check girl
as a matter of course.

A nod to beauty
and it's mastery
of the moment.
Its discretion,
fury,
and the obvious ways

it jolts, lures
and leaves you
broken. Whole
unlike before.

Left of the Green Lampshade

It was funny grooming myself
in isolation. Do I shave? Do I shower?
Do I tuck in my shirt?
Do I tilt the screen just left of the green lampshade
for best effect? Do I mirror myself
or go commando
And let those of you
on the other end
of the string
See for yourselves
if I hid the weed
or drank all the wine.
Okay welcome! Here's the house.
Did these days sneak up on you too
because we all ignored
the rearview warning
That objects are closer than they seem?
Are all the little anxieties from outside adapting,
like anything wishing a lifespan would,
making you anxious inside?
Are you making your days fruitful?
Planting seeds? Cleaning house?
Throwing out the old?
Whatever it was that bound us then,
when now is all that matters.

where the light sneaks in

The psychic took my personal check and I
quickly questioned all her projections.
Surely she knew my grifter past before predicting
Ten weeks on The Times Top Ten,
Amazon Prime's Big Pick.

Have you read my stuff
it's freaking depressing I said.
A curt evaluation I'll concede but
I don't see stars anymore
just bullet holes where the light sneaks in.

We need your truth she said
and I thought: *Wow!*
What a promo blurb that'd make.
Let Kirkus charge me now!

This country ain't piss she said
lending credence to my last submissions,
heft to my whole oeuvre.
Can I quote ya I asked w/a grimace,
my standard scowl of the day.
Twenty six ninety nine she said
w/o fanfare or delight.

Combustible Flannel

In a bar I call home
The violence of victims
is good for a laugh.
The armored police
set up shop.
The shooting lists
are selling well.
Elvis appears
in combustible flannel.
God and monkey
steal the sky.
Cyclone kids
cavort w/rage.
Can't relate
w/o suspicion.
Our anthems carry
their own indictment.
No one cares
the Earth is burning.
I spend my last penny
In a bar I call home.

the hour before

Odd Tango was an atheist
after the war.
What choice was there?
Electroshock? Brown Crystal?
A calming agent
every four hours
didn't cease
the darkness.
Didn't make
his hairpin hold
any less shakier
than the hour before
the flashlight crapped
and the jungle
cranked to ten.

Counting corpses
rides hard the minutes.
The Wabash shakes
he inherited from his father
didn't make rest much easier
or peaceful. In fact it
agitated the hour.
The hour before
every four hours.

Two Miles North

I know by the dumpsters
this little town juggles
boxed wine and take out
from Imperial Geisha
two miles north on 29.
where another black kid's
gone down.

Legend Holds

What the ladies said about Billy the Kid
was true: He hid under petticoats often
after coaxing the red dog sun from their loins.
He'd rest in the Sierra Blanca,
reading dime store novels
with a grin that frayed at the edges.

His dusty boots, his crooked hats
cast shadows on the noose. Until one day
when some great love, or its proximity,
divided his bones for sport.

w/Raphael Kosek & Will Nixon

it was an evening

it was an evening of burlap
and bemusement. Ironic
but nothing unusual: Liberal arts
and wine. I forged my father's
name on the loan.
In the morning
she woke up shopping

The Reason You Dreamt (*after ra*)

The reason you dreamt. Of wise men. Playing pinochle.
    On stilts.
Is because. It was my   dream. Absconded from my head
    by Baku,
the dream thief. Who goes. About. The world. Taking
    whatever's not
nailed down. Yours. Mine. Your mama's. Your great aunt's
    green teeth

Your father's suit of blue.

You could. Say. You had. The craziest dream but. You didn't.
You had mine. While I, in Weehauken. Had yours. Caught.
    myself.
Got up to feed the cat. And you can ask for your dreams back
    but. It's like. Immigrant children crying. And tonight. Is
    no. exception.

In the Grey Light

In the grey light
of the East Side
Freaks gather
the garden party.
The wine ain't cheap
And I can't tell
if I've blown
the sure double play
or if the ump should be
tending tables.

In the grey light
of the East Side
I'm walking the mulberry
and redbud. The air hushed, flawless.
The river a hug of diamonds.

flaws apparent

Given how the world's gone
since his going, it's kind of fitting
his old mantle clock chimed its last
eighteen years to the day
of his last hour.

But that was him, of course.
Always present. Like that day his rosary,
hanging from my rearview broke
as I was topping Miller Hill.
And I knew. And I knew.
Then the call. And I knew

He wanted me to know
he'd be here atop this mountain
wishing I wasn't smoking weed
but happy I am who I was:
the flaws apparent.
A man reviving.

Elephant, galleon, whips, and chains

Guns and bombs. Cannons and spears. Daggers, pistols, swords and rifles.
Muskets, bayonets. Pocket knives, box cutters. Scissors, buzz bombs, sticks.
Hydrogen, halogen, Fire 'n ice. Asymmetrical. Hypersonic. Flamethrowers,
stones and tanks. Gatlin's Patent 36836. Chlorine, napalm, mustard, tear gas.
Catapult. Submarine. Missiles. Drones. Atomic. Scatter. Blast.
The Betty, the Huey, the M-16. Fokkers, Sopwiths, chariots and Jeeps.
Meathook. Bat. The bow and arrow. Maxim's design and Louie's three-0-three caliber. Mortars. Rapiers. Sabres and shortsword.
Pole ax and mace. The rake. The plane. The battle ax and flail.
Pike and lance, scythe and chakram. The dogs of war.
   The camels.
The elephant and galleon. Gauntlet. Castle. Whips and chains.
Blowguns, tachi, and deer horn. Push dagger, Swiss dagger.
Lockheed and Glock. Boeing. Grumman. BAE.
Rockwell. Honeywell. Saab. GE. Raytheon. Rolls Royce and General Atomic. United Engine. Springfield. Airbus. Konsberg Gruppen.
I-net worms and Winchester. Zero Sum, flintlock. The claw of Archimedes.
Remington. Colt. Tsar Bomb and the Judas Cradle beats 'em all.

fuckin town

Crackpipe Joe recalled the old days fondly:
It all happens at once in the Bronx
he says. *The physics impaired*
prepare to park. A ground floor crone
calls the garbage can Bill 'n
kicks a cabbage to the curb.
That's just how it is in dust city
he says, mottling back to June 88
When he and Tessa nodded on the Interborough
and woke up snuggling a rare Jasper Johns.
A Neo-Dada abstract she said
And she knew too, having doyened downtown
before . . . well, y'know before her tone became
more baleful 'n narcotic'n all this wasn't here
'n all that wasn't either.

See the ambient index at the center of the swirl?
she queried. *And of course I did. We were both*
cool young pedestals upon which art rested.
It's the only thing of beauty we own she said.
But I wanted to hock it 'n keep the good times rolling
but women, y'know, they have their ways.
So we've piped it from borough to borough
to the old Plymouth parked on one seventy eight.
Waiting for the right price
'n beat it from this fuckin town.

Brubeck's Bar #6

Straight up baby straight up
like the blues and the ramparts.
Blakey. Birdland. Brubeck's Bar.
Straight up baby straight up
on the 7 to Fulton under cloud shade
and shale which will tell its own in time.

Straight up baby straight up
and he's on the phone fighting about her period,
who fucked who and the whole bar knows it,
par for a city under surveillance I guess.
And I fondly recall when my parents
would pull me in close if someone came
down the street or rode this same #6
yelling at invisible strangers.
Talking to themselves in a tone that,
to be perfectly honest,
stifles the bare rail cry. The infallible hum
you hear on each corner
that returns my thoughts to Heaven
and if it rains there is it cold?
Is parking a challenge up there too?

Brushing Light Snow

Another story has it that
it really was the same dream
w/the same outcome: Jarrett '72.
Today. Brushing light snow.
Our footprints merging
into one w/all the dreamy gauze
attached. The handmade cards and
Minton's. A bit south of the Yonkers line
t' Harlem
t' hear Charlie P and C
and Kenny behind Monk
who was behind no one
That third week in May
whatever the year when
the motion of Heaven
moved us all to the point
of you saying yes
and me saying yes
and Max saying yes
Taking the music
through thick, thin,
sickness, and poor.
To Jarrett today
brushing light snow.

Ill-Fitting Suit

It was like it wanted no part
of the rotund trumpeter
who pulled it from its hanger
from where? Barney's? Syms?
Macy's Basement?
And chose to wear it
on this night on this stage.
It struggled to break free
from this portly player:
Crinkled, leadened, almost pallid.
It just didn't fit and everyone in the house
knew it. How could they not in the spotlight
as it were: The ballad smooth, elegiac.
The suit? Not so much. Even the trumpet
was like *Dude, lose the garb.*
The tailor never meant it to fit this way:
Ungraceful as deflation. Baggy, inchoate
and so shiny too!
Like a latter day Van Morrison
flailing in a Brooks Brothers cut.
The sleeves are too long and if
the cuffs had fingers they'd be gloves
on his pudgy claw.

It doesn't help that he's hassling
w/his valves all night and
his pants don't fit either.
Un-ironed, unhip, uncouth.
Bunching at the knees and the ankles
like a lawless coat of indeterminate color
and shiny like the jacket but not a suit.
Two pieces of attire never attended.
Never intended to compliment or complete
on this night, this stage
in New York, New York.

Pittsburg

I shit, shower, shave 'n
shove off for Pittsburg.
Where everything beeps at me
derisively: Gas pump. Smart phone.
Toothbrush. Vape pen.
Microwave kills the salmon!

If I had any balls at all
like Uncle Hank opposed the wheel,
I'd smash them with a rock.
But I wean on leisure
and regret my vote
like all good citizens do.

In a Walmart In Kentucky

I'm in a Walmart in Kentucky
   (why I'll never know)
Reading Andy Martin's last letter
about a girl w/skin like lotto balls.
Rife w/pills he goes on to say
that we condemn every besieged democracy
but our own. That there are things we do and
things we live w/. And if flies are karma
we'd best like eating shit.

Scuff Marks

Between chandelier and bandstand
we chart our existence never expecting
the roof to fall, the floor to cave.
Clean as a whistle.
But there's always some spit to a whistle
just ask my dad, the town's champ whistler.
Though he barely remembers that now.
Alzheimer's y'know. Some sort of dementia
or brain arthritis. They never really explain these things,
like most things, I guess.
Until, well,
just until.

Breaching Aristotle *(month4)*

So what new scab
do I pick today
to open our discussion?
Month 4's been a drag
hasn't it? Staring at bonobos
staring back - breaching Aristotle,
bellicose and belligerent
And dragging the bygone
w/arthritic hands.
Harsh percussions
precedes nquiry
and I can't wait (to be honest)
to hear all about it.
But not today!
Today's put aside
to hear Monk move
and give us
(in his own disturbed grace)
the inside track
on the outside joke
And how all of this came to be
(for the most part)
a world of our own
incompetence. Fools of the realm
w/o benchmark. Primate vs. primate
rising up the ranks.

brushfire

w/the breath
(of burnt tires)
the voice
(of God)
never allows
(the night)
to darken

Ballad of Black Bean Johnson

On the corner of Willis and one-four-nine
from a Barcalounger outside Johnny's,
Black Bean Johnson held court.
You take your best shit on the day you die
he tells us neophyte urchins.

He spoke like God
if they spoke the same language.
His old man breath. His old man eyes.
His dirty v-neck
torn from the hunt.

We are the sum of our secrets he howls
at the women walking home from Hearns.
And we paid attention! Rapt attention. We had to.
They didn't teach this shit in school
no matter how fancy the parochial setting
or broken the brick and mortar.

Captain of his corner,
we wondered how someone so wise
could live so spare. So bare,
so undisputed.
A coup is afoot
he warned the rain.

E suspended

The fleeting cellist found herself
lost among the woodwinds.
Bumping into music stands,
bruising chamber mates.

Barely taller than her burden,
like herself, made of wood
and glue. Pegbox and scroll.

The harpsichord's chair is deserted
but everyone's getting out of town.
This gig has run its course and if
the wolf tones are true,
leaner days are nearing.
And New York is no place for players
who cannot hold their own.

Liberal, Kansas

They were gonna kill Somalis
'cos who's better at immigrant rage
than jerk-off white guys
goaded by God w/guns?
Pending domestic charges and
'scripts they can't refill 'cos
the God-damm government checks
ain't in.

They were gonna kill Somalis 'cos
that's what patriots do: Kill those who don't
look like them. Talk like them.
Believe like them. Eat n drink n
piss n fuck like them.

They were gonna kill Somalis 'cos
they're douche-bags and
America's like that now:
Ignorant. Inhospitable. A backwash town
on a washed-out map. Lined w/refugees
coast to coast.

Light Between Buildings

A lot of times
  (when rainbows preside)
I find myself dancing
through God's good hour
w/the same side step
my father passed down
and limbo into the light
between buildings.

'Cos what else does
a street kid have
but his own longitude,
  (his latitude)
and a whole lot of stage
between him
and the waiting rain.

Man w/the Giant Camera

   The man w/the giant camera
rolls into town on ambrotype rails.
   His young assistant juggles
old equipment, strange tools,
small plates of scratched glass, tin, silver
   the Graflex 4x5. The light
catches her eye. For a longish moment
   the negative burns. Like acid
images blur. Like gelatin,
   like egg whites.
And the light recalls
    back home: where the land and the wife
deliver new yields. Hold the albumen.
   Subtle, dark, and fine.

Eve

Like a cueball w/o english
she edits an art-house magazine.
Like a puck in play
she bounces off the boards.
Like a hole in your pocket
she loses the same stuff.
Like the distance between us
she can't fill w/grace.

Fuzzy Circles

Holding the venom between us,
the poem that ran out of ink
has a deep, rich backstory
you can dance to
and a final line
I'm rather enthralled by.

  (remember us the better who we are)

Humor is essential
in these times.
Blue tarps bungeed
along the East River.
Shiftless study
pursued w/o looking.
Self made men

  (and women, beleaguered)

is my American recollection
not yours.. I get it.
I just can't cotton how
you get from A to B
w/o God, the cartographer,
drawing fuzzy circles.

  (and the skies are not cloudy all day)

Shamed Angels

I never thought
I'd ever read
a magazine
w/Linda Ronstadt
and 'rhoid relief
on the cover
proclaiming
in extra wide Calibri
the need for a pill or a pet
or barnacle extraction.
Eye and ear and
nose repair.
Chronic hints
our hour nears.

She was so gorgeous
w/eyes like wet silk moons
and a voice that shamed angels.
Now it's lasix and remedy.
Stroke and contrition.
Each our own ache and pain and
burden. Dog-earring pages
lest we forget.

in my car of feathers

In my car of feathers
the great handling of cash
takes us parallel
the big screen
as the former
feeds the latter
and the smokers
miss the good stuff.

It goes so fast
the slack eyed maven interred
as to the whereabouts
of the 9:15 susurrus

Fish Talk

Born in Paterson
(New Jersey, that is)
and commissioned by the Navy in '46
to pry into all matters
of the marine heart,
Marie Poland Fish
heard tadpoles tattle.
Insisted kelp could talk.

Codfish frenzy after spawning!
Whales sing! Krill pertain!
Eels chortle! Cod refrain.

They called her Bobbi
after her 'do.
(its sharp bounce
so bewitching)

The living make a common scream
she often would reply.

Data spill

Under the briny assumption
> that

every imported anxiety is,
> in fact,

its own love child,
Can we not
> all concur

that every
> data spill

is
> in fact

a slow motion
> fuse

to a body
> about to

what?
> Take a turn?

Find a muse?
> Birth a nation?

Burn a flag?

And that

despite

our best

try

the fish fry

unravels

in verse,

verdict,

and villanelle

riven w/grievance

and spoil

9/10's of Tuesday

In the valley of displaced nouns,
rain falls w/a zombie fervor
9/10's of the time.
And a tenth takes a while
to confess so

If you haven't guessed by now
this is one of those poems
I get stuck in often.
Unsure how to worm my way out
and time my escape
before you catch on
and turn the page
w/distraction.

Walking Awosting

We re-arrange nature
for a very short time.
The tree re-occurs.
The wind replaces seed.
Rivers over-run their banks
to reclaim the land we've taken.

We try to replenish our stock
but to no lasting avail.
Nature accepts our intrusion.
Absorbs our attempts at mastery
and advances her greater plan.

We can only watch,
jiggle the handle,
and die. That is all
we do.

The Merchant's Receipt

It's the perfect killing machine
I'm told. *I'll take it* I say
signing the merchant's receipt.

That was easy. I get more hassle
from Hulu. And what's not to like
about a state made weapon
guaranteed to garner
a whole lot of airtime.
Analysis. Punditry.

College sweethearts sobbing.
The class nurse swearing
she warned your mom.
Cousins from Bumfuck
recall lone behaviors.

Strapped w/two thousand rounds
and ultra HD, I can beat the mass tally
if I'm on my game n I am
like in a movie where all the extras die
like roaches after the credits fade.

suit of blue

Here at Find - A- Grave
we do. Yours, mine,
your mama's. Old blues dudes
and new guitars. Your bird.
Your dog. Your hamster turtle
garden snake. Your sister's remaining foot.
Her third husband's green sweater.
Your father's suit of blue
and his hidden tools.
Your brother's magazines
and your great aunt's teeth.
Your uncle's arm and his first born's
crooked grin. All who served
and whom they served.
Silver, wood.
Stone and sanction.
The fractions
we think ours
to keep.

pissin' 'round the lilies

Humor, the red assed hawk
circles the pines
as if waiting for me
to fall midstream
while marking my line
so Norman, the groundhog
won't make a full meal
of my opulent buds.

By the feeder
Tweak chuckles
at the flaccid lance
I hold against Nature.
Joyfully losing
my grip on it all.

Rejection 629

I really don't care

what you think.

I'll keep writing

disturbing notes

if only

to beguile myself

and my remnant aunt

confined to a wheelchair

who glowers when

I read aloud.

Points to the sky

and tells me it's raining.

Tells me

It's time

and wheels away.

Mike's poetry and music reviews have been published globally but with little reportable income. Full length collections include *mooncussers,* (Luchador Press 2022); *AmericanMental,* (Luchador Press 2020). *Blue Fan Whirring* (Nirala Press, 2018) Anthologies: *Calling All Poets 20th Anniversary Anthology,* (CAPS Press); *Reflecting Pool: Poets & the Creative Process* (Codhill Press, 2018); *Like Light: 25 Years of Poetry & Prose* (Bright Hill Press, 2018) among others. Now in its 23rd year, he serves as President of Calling All Poets. CD reviews online at All About Jazz and Lightwood. Mike serves as chairman of the curated Music Fan Series, Rosendale Theater. He hosts New Jazz Excursions alternating Saturdays 10am-12pm on WIOX 91.3FM, Roxbury, NY. Streaming live at wioxradio.org. *The Rock n Roll Curmudgeon* appeared in *Rhythm and News Magazine,* 1996-2003.

www.ingramcontent.com/pod-product-compliance
Lightning Source LLC
Chambersburg PA
CBHW030137100526
44592CB00011B/929